MUSICAL INSTRUMENTS

Keyboards

Ruth Daly

LET'S READ

AV²
BY WEIGL™

ADDED VALUE · AUDIO VISUAL

www.av2books.com

AV² provides enriched content that supplements and complements this book. Weigl's AV² books strive to create inspired learning and engage young minds in a total learning experience.

Your AV² Media Enhanced books come alive with...

Go to **www.av2books.com**, and enter this book's unique code.

BOOK CODE

LBE47388

AV² by Weigl brings you media enhanced books that support active learning.

Audio
Listen to sections of the book read aloud.

Video
Watch informative video clips.

Embedded Weblinks
Gain additional information for research.

Try This!
Complete activities and hands-on experiments.

Key Words
Study vocabulary, and complete a matching word activity.

Quizzes
Test your knowledge.

Slide Show
View images and captions, and prepare a presentation.

... and much, much more!

Published by AV² by Weigl
350 5th Avenue, 59th Floor   New York, NY   10118
Website: www.av2books.com

Library of Congress Control Number: 2017956493

ISBN 978-1-4896-7275-9 (hardcover)
ISBN 978-1-4896-7310-7 (softcover)
ISBN 978-1-4896-7276-6 (multi-user eBook)

Printed in the United States of America in Brainerd, Minnesota
1 2 3 4 5 6 7 8 9 0 21 20 19 18 17

112017
102517

Project Coordinator: John Willis   Designer: Nick Newton

Weigl acknowledges Alamy, Getty Images, and iStock as the primary image suppliers for this title.

MUSICAL
INSTRUMENTS

Keyboards

In this book, you will learn about

keyboards

what they are

how you play them

and much more!

3

4

Strike the keys. Push the buttons. Hear the different sounds of the keyboard!

5

A keyboard is an electric instrument. It looks like a piano. A keyboard has black and white keys. It also has different buttons.

A piano has 88 keys. Keyboards can have 61, 76, or 88 keys.

People strike the keys with their fingers. This makes sounds called notes. The black keys make notes called sharps and flats.

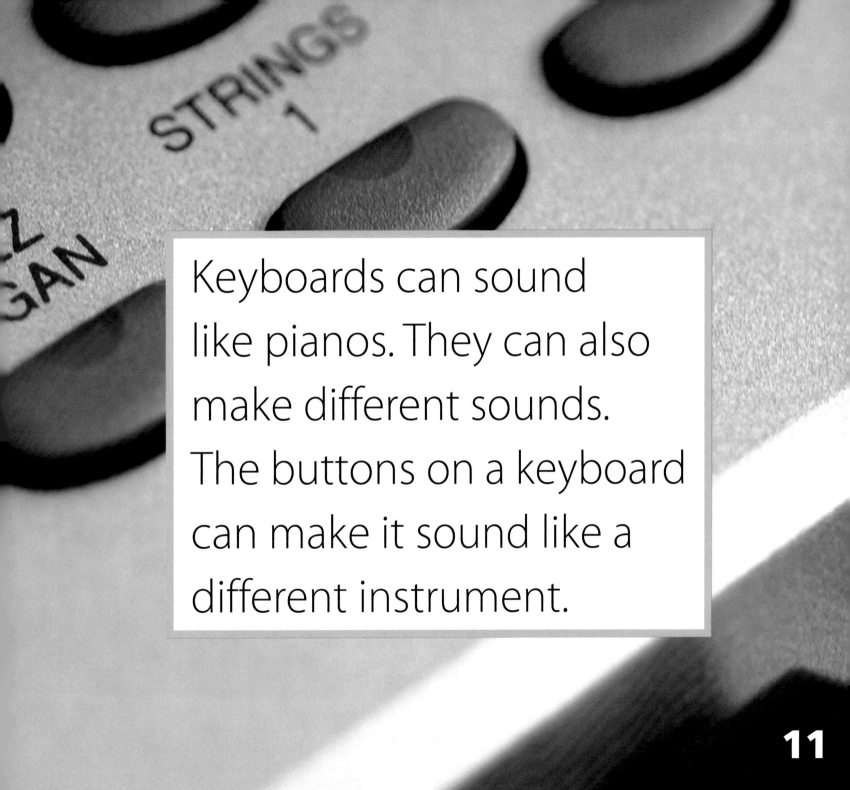

Keyboards can sound like pianos. They can also make different sounds. The buttons on a keyboard can make it sound like a different instrument.

Pressing the keys makes an electric signal. The signal passes to an amplifier and a speaker. This makes a noise.

13

14

Most keyboards are made of plastic. This means that they are not as heavy as pianos.

People played instruments like keyboards long ago. These instruments were not electric. One early keyboard instrument was called the harpsichord.

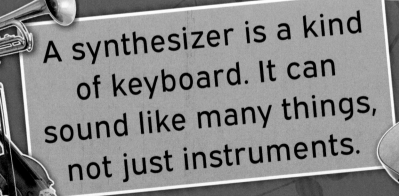

A synthesizer is a kind of keyboard. It can sound like many things, not just instruments.

Keyboards are used in many kinds of music. Gospel music uses keyboards. They can be used in rock music, too.

A keytar is a guitar-shaped keyboard. It is used in pop music.

Many people like to play the keyboard. Some people have a keyboard in their home. They can play any kind of music they enjoy.

See what you have learned about keyboards.

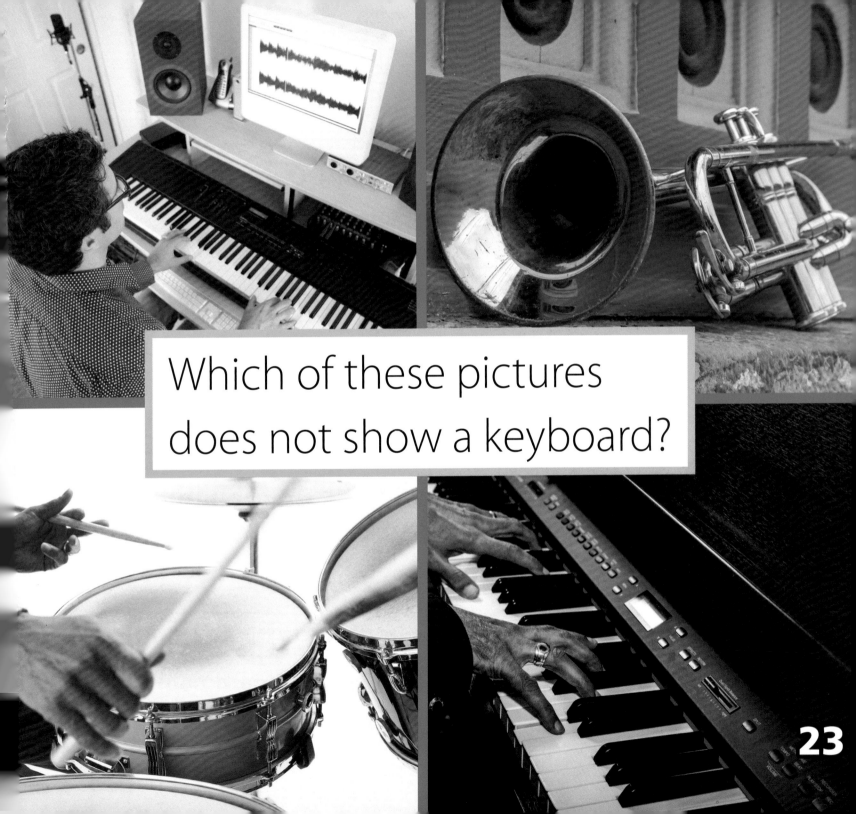

Which of these pictures does not show a keyboard?

KEY WORDS

Research has shown that as much as 65 percent of all written material published in English is made up of 300 words. These 300 words cannot be taught using pictures or learned by sounding them out. They must be recognized by sight. This book contains 50 common sight words to help young readers improve their reading fluency and comprehension. This book also teaches young readers several important content words, such as proper nouns. These words are paired with pictures to aid in learning and improve understanding.

Page	Sight Words First Appearance
5	different, hear, of, sounds, the
6	a, also, an, and, can, has, have, is, it, like, looks, or, white
9	makes, people, their, this, with
11	on, they
12	to
15	are, as, made, means, most, not, that
16	just, kind, long, many, one, these, things, was, were
19	be, in, too, used
20	any, home, play, some

Page	Content Words First Appearance
5	buttons, keyboard, keys
6	instrument, piano
9	fingers, flats, notes, sharps
12	amplifier, noise, signal, speaker
15	plastic
16	harpsichord, synthesizer
19	gospel music, guitar, keytar, pop music, rock music